What Our Readers Have Said...

"The Pinpoint Training Series delivers information that could be used in a lot different areas."

•

"Applicable and valid. The information is good."

•

"I like this because I can take them with me to read at a convenient time. I feel the little time I have to spend in the office is best use on activities that directly relate to revenue opportunities. I like the short amount of time it takes to keep up with these."

•

"I like the fact that the format allows the books to be reviewed as time permits. All work has been conducted on personal, evening/weekend time."

•

"My thought is that the real value of these books comes into effect when doing the action plans."

•

"The challenge when I think a specific topic does not apply is to find a way to make it apply."

•

"Short and sweet. These books are easy to comprehend."

•

"These books are very easy to read and clearly outlined."

•

"I have enjoyed reading these books. They are relevant to today's work environment and the ongoing change in the way we manage our workforce."

•

"I believe the contents of the Pinpoint series are excellent. It causes one to reflect on the daily dynamics in working with oneself as well as with management and peers."

•

"Most of the information in these would help an open-minded management person, or an inexperienced management person."

•

"These books will pay for the time that I am investing. There are numerous good ideas that will streamline what I do and how I do it."

•

"All and all I think the Pinpoint series is a good program. I know other people I would love to have something like this. I think a lot of the suggestions are very useful, and can be applicable to everyday situations. If nothing else it's a good reference guide to fall back upon if a situation arises in the future."

•

"These books reinforce many concepts that I have learned through seminars, schooling and other programs. For myself, it serves as a constant learning tool that keeps me on top of the issues that many of us encounter every day."

•

"All in all, I think you have good training books. It helps everyone to review these materials, it serves as a good reminder to us on how to conduct ourselves."

•

"The information is valuable in these books."

•

Resolving Customer Service Problems

Pinpoint Sales Management Skill Development Training Series

TIMOTHY F. BEDNARZ

MAJORIUM
BUSINESS PRESS

Pinpoint Sales Management Skill Development Training Series
"Resolving Customer Service Problems"
Timothy F. Bednarz

Graphic design: Monika Pawlak

Majorium Business Press
2025 Main Street
Stevens Point, WI 54481
715.342.1018 • 800.654.4935

ISBN 978-1-882181-54-4

Printed in the United States of America

Introduction

The Pinpoint Sales Management Skill Development Training Series is designed for targeted training and education regarding increased improvement in a specific skill or competency.

Each book within this series is designed to be easy to use, understand and apply to your job. It can be used as a basis for training individuals, as a discussion guide or as a personal training tool.

Each chapter within this book discusses a specific concept. When you have completed all eight chapters you should have a 360° perspective of the topic.

Additionally, each chapter is divided into specific sections:

- The first section provides you with an overview of the topic
- The Implications section discusses why the concept is important, and why it is important to learn and apply.
- The Strategies, Tips & Techniques to Apply section teaches how to use and apply the particular concept to your work.
- The Points to Ponder section gives you something to think about or to be discussed with a group setting. These are questions not meant to be immediately answered, but to be pondered over time.
- The Training Activity section provides you with the tools to transfer what you have learned to your job. It is designed to help create an action plan to effectively apply the concept.

Each of the topics in this series is time-tested and proven in the marketplace. They have been used by thousands of employees as training tools. Many of the users have commented that what made these books valuable, was the ability to refer to them when a problem surfaced. They indicated that they remembered reading about the exact problem. They referred back to these books and found an appropriate solution.

You will find them equally valuable as a resource in your professional development library.

Table of Contents

LEARNING OBJECTIVES:

- To identify the use and application of customer service methods and techniques.
- To determine why customer service is essential to overall success.
- To build a strong customer service support team.
- To effectively monitor and evaluate customer service performance.

1

What Causes Most of Your Problems?

Every problem has a cause. Unfortunately, most real causes are often masked by symptoms; but with the proper problem solving techniques, the symptoms will point to the direct cause. A problem whose cause is understood is already half solved. Effective sales managers will discover the cause and then remove it, which ultimately solves the problem.

Most problems generally fall into four major categories: functional problems, misapplication, human problems, and problems based upon emotion. As it turns out, 80% of problems stem from emotional causes.

IMPLICATIONS – WHAT THIS MEANS TO YOU

When sales managers are confronted with a customer-related problem, they must seek to understand its cause and gain the proper insight, facts and information to solve it. To remain competitive they need to take responsibility for the problem and then resolve it to the customer's satisfaction.

People have a natural tendency when confronted with a problem to become emotional and defensive and to place the blame on others. Most customers are used to dealing with this attitude. Therefore, when a company takes responsibility to solve a problem and assure customer satisfaction, they gain a competitive advantage.

STRATEGIES, TIPS & TECHNIQUES TO APPLY

When confronted with a problem, sales managers should immediately do four things:

- Find out what happened.
- Determine what should have happened.
- Find out what specifically went wrong.
- Settle on what it will take to solve the problem to the customer's satisfaction.

The most common causes of problems tend to be:

- *Functional* – The product or service didn't work right.
- *Misapplication* – The customer didn't use it correctly.
- *Human problems* – The product wasn't manufactured or maintained properly.
- *Problems based upon emotion* – The problem makes people look bad in front of others or causes them some sort of undue stress.

Most problems sales managers encounter aren't logical; indeed, they can often be based upon a customer's ego or emotions. Customers often put themselves in a position where their egos won't allow them to back down or accept a logical solution if they think that it was their fault. The best approach to counteracting this type of problem is for the sales manager to take personal responsibility and ownership of it, and guarantee customer satisfaction. This effectively neutralizes emotional responses.

As sales managers begin to formulate a resolution to a problem, they should be cognizant of the costs an unresolved problem brings to the company. They must also consider the long-term implications of an acceptable solution. Some factors to consider when evaluating the real costs of a solution should include:

- What will a satisfactory solution cost?
- What value will future purchases from this customer deliver?
- Analyze how this customer will impact future business (in general)

based on the happiness, or lack thereof, with the solution offered.

Sales managers should be also cognizant of the fact that 91% of unhappy customers will never buy from them again whereas an all-out effort to resolve customer complaints yields an 82-95% retention rate. A sales manager must always keep one fact at the forefront: It costs about five times more to attract a new customer than it does to keep an old one.

POINTS TO PONDER — SOMETHING TO THINK ABOUT

1. Have you ever viewed your customer's problems with skepticism? Have you ever felt they lied to you or were trying to take advantage of you?
2. Do you boldly defend your position if the customer is wrong? Has this position helped or hurt your sales efforts?

TRAINING ACTIVITY — APPLICATION & ACTION PLAN

1. Establish a formal plan for handling customer complaints.
2. Identify the initial actions you will take, the strategies you will use to resolve the problem, and how you intend to follow up in order to ensure customer satisfaction.

2

Facilitating and Eliciting Customer Feedback

Surveys reflect that for every customer complaint a company receives, there are approximately 25 other customers who remain silent. Some of these silent customers prefer to quickly find another supplier rather than resolve their problems. In other instances, they will silently suffer until they cannot tolerate the problem any longer, will finally break ties with the guilty vendor without any hope of a future business relationship, and actively work to harm their business in order to teach them a lesson.

Rather than see complaints exclusively as problems, sales managers must embrace them and actively encourage customers to come forth and be vocal about them. Effective sales managers will view complaints as golden opportunities to highlight their company's supreme level of service in actively and effectively resolving problems.

IMPLICATIONS – WHAT THIS MEANS TO YOU

When customers analyze the complaint process, they often realize personal shortcomings. Many feel unable to express themselves adequately. Others feel uncomfortable, seeing themselves as a potential problem to the sales representative; they wish to complain only to attain the satisfaction they were promised, but simply cannot handle being seen as a nuisance. Some customers may be insecure and cannot get past the discomfort of dealing with unknown individuals. Still others believe it comes down to a "me against them" conflict, feeling that in order to get the desired results they must muster up enough courage to aggressively take on the company and its employees.

It is important for sales managers to understand that the majority of customers are uncomfortable with registering a complaint. Sales managers must ensure that their people are watchful for potential problem situations with customers and can remedy any issues before they become major. Salespeople must constantly query their customers about their satisfaction levels. In fact, when customers are encouraged to complain in this manner, salespeople can use each situation to foster and nurture their business.

STRATEGIES, TIPS & TECHNIQUES TO APPLY

Sales managers should take the time to explore what it is like to complain to a supervisor. Most would probably begin the process by evaluating their communication skills. Then, time is spent deciding the best way to communicate effectively. No doubt, many experience some sort of fear when thinking about the potential intimidation that comes with confronting a superior. At this point, careful consideration is often necessary to weigh the possible risks versus rewards of making a complaint. Many customers experience the same feelings when they need to complain about a problem.

Customers are also very reluctant to invest the substantial time that it often takes to resolve a problem: it is inconvenient, adds extra work to their often already busy schedule, and is difficult at best. Many customers wonder, "Is it really worth the energy?"

Sales managers should keep in mind that when customers complain they have certain expectations:

Heard and Listened to Respectfully

Customers want to be respected. A salesperson quickly undermines his or her credibility by minimizing what the customer has to say. Often sales or support people consider a problem minor, yet it is major in the eyes of the customer.

Salespeople should listen respectfully, ask questions to clarify the situation and, if necessary, allow the customer to vent his or her frustrations.

Served Efficiently and Considerately

Companies must value their customers. Sales and support people who hide behind policy manuals or bureaucratic red tape to mask their inability or refusal to resolve a problem will find their business floundering. Customers expect problems to occur; they just want them resolved with as little confrontation as possible.

Fast Action

Customer surveys indicate that the most loyal customers are those who experienced a problem with a vendor but had their issues quickly and pleasantly resolved. The sales manager who understands this correlation is one who recognizes that a complaint represents yet another chance to serve the customer. Complaints allow individual salespeople to shine. Solving problems effectively and quickly actually works to strengthen relationships.

An Atmosphere Built on Mutual Trust

When customers experience a problem, they have some basic expectations: to have the problem fixed quickly at the supplier's expense without hassle or confrontation. Often these expectations are unspoken. Yet, the situation can quickly deteriorate when the sales manager's company fails to meet these expectations. As time goes by and the problem remains unresolved, the customer's trust in the company rapidly diminishes.

Important and Valued

Customers want to know that their business is valued and that they are important to the sales manager and his or her company. When the sales manager adequately addresses the concerns discussed in this lesson, the customer feels valued. If any of these concerns are left unresolved, then problems are guaranteed to continue.

Sales managers should know that the closure of a customer complaint is just as important as solving the problem. Closure is the final step that ensures a positive resolution to all of the customer's questions, negative attitudes and frustrations; done right, this cements the customer's loyalty.

A sales manager's attitude toward customer complaints can work for or against them. If a manager's policies and/or salespeople dissuade customers from complaining, it becomes automatic for the company to continuously lose customers. Sales managers need to ensure that their people actively encourage customers to voice complaints. Everyone should see complaints as a positive process rather than a negative experience.

POINTS TO PONDER — SOMETHING TO THINK ABOUT

1. Do you make it easy for your customers to voice their complaints and concerns? What actions do you take?
2. What is your typical attitude toward a customer who complains? Is your attitude reflected in how your salespeople handle the complaint and deal with the customer?

TRAINING ACTIVITY — APPLICATION & ACTION PLAN

Design a plan to meet the concerns of your customers.

1. Create two columns on a sheet of paper.
2. List the customer concerns outlined in this lesson.
3. Next to each, state several new strategies you can use to address each one.

3

Taking Control of Complaints

Complaints are inevitable in sales. Problems and issues constantly arise. Yet, despite operating in a highly competitive and volatile environment that is extremely sensitive to economic changes—and thus at high risk for customer attrition—it is surprising how many sales managers take a lackadaisical approach to problem solving.

How sales personnel handle complaints determines the future of customer relationships with their company. Poor handling of problems and complaints can result in the instant loss of a sale and the customer.

IMPLICATIONS – WHAT THIS MEANS TO YOU

When a customer has a complaint, they want it quickly addressed. No one expects perfection, but the sales department's response to a problem has two possible consequences. On the one hand, they can cause additional frustration and pain for the customer. As a result, the customer will ultimately seek out someone else who can help—namely, a competitor. The second possibility is a happy and satisfied customer impressed with the speed and efficiency with which his or her problem was resolved. These customers will be even more loyal to the company because it is clear that their business is valued.

It is important for sales managers to realize that when a complaint arises their people have critical choices to make. These choices have long-term repercussions for the company and can spell success or failure.

STRATEGIES, TIPS & TECHNIQUES TO APPLY

When the company is confronted with a customer complaint, the sales manager's goal is to have his or her people arrive at a positive solution in a controlled and natural way. Discussed below are several aspects required to attain this positive outcome.

Listen to What Is Being Said

When a customer is making a complaint, sales managers must ensure that their people restrain any emotional and defensive responses that are typical initial reactions in such situations. They must maintain control of their emotions and remain objective. Good solutions can only be crafted in an impartial, logical environment.

Individuals must make sure they are really focusing on and hearing what the customer is saying. They should listen carefully and observe nonverbal cues in the customer's face, vocal tone and body language. They must "read between the lines" to interpret what is actually being communicated by the customer. It also helps to listen for keywords, needs, desires and expected outcomes, all of which serve to convey what the customer truly wants. The primary focus should be on developing a clear and objective picture of the customer's actual needs.

Demonstrate Appreciation and Interest

Complaints are opportunities for sales managers and their company. It gives them the chance to highlight their company's excellent customer service. After developing a clear picture of the customer's actual needs, sales managers should ensure that their people thank the customer for informing them about the problem and demonstrate their sincere interest in quickly resolving it.

While this whole process may seem unimportant, only a small number of customers actually complain. The majority, in fact, quietly walk away and look for another supplier. A complaining customer thus gives the company a unique opportunity.

Probe for Solutions

Customers will often suggest more modest solutions to their own problem than a sales manager would. Therefore, before offering a solution that is too extreme, sales managers should have their people probe the customer in detail to determine what specifically needs to be done to resolve the problem.

Those who take the time to develop a clear and objective picture of the customer's needs should have little difficulty probing the customer for a solution. Once the individual knows what is important to the customer, it is easy to pursue agreeable and focused avenues of interest and concern.

Agree to a Solution

Before individuals leave a meeting with an angry customer, they should recap the entire discussion and agree to the next action step. The most important moment is getting the customer to agree that the solution crafted will satisfy him or her; the meeting absolutely cannot end until this critical step is taken.

When sales managers have their people follow up with the customer to provide details, they should offer specific information about who will implement the solution, when it will be delivered, and how it will work to resolve the customer's problem satisfactorily. After the solution is employed, the person dealing with the customer should ensure that everything promised by the company was delivered to the customer's complete satisfaction.

POINTS TO PONDER — SOMETHING TO THINK ABOUT

1. Have you ever lost customers as a result of how your company handled a complaint?
2. Do you view complaints as opportunities or annoyances?

TRAINING ACTIVITY – APPLICATION & ACTION PLAN

1. Detail how you defuse an angry and/or hostile customer situation.
2. Compare and contrast your solution with the steps outlined in this lesson.

4

What Would Be Fair?

At one time or another, sales managers need to deal with very aggressive and emotional customers. These individuals are extremely angry and openly hostile about a problem caused by the sales manager's company. Their reasons can include poor quality, slow delivery, a lack of service or poor installation.

Often these customers are under substantial pressure caused by downsized staffs, increased responsibilities and "just-in-time" ordering systems. They cling to a delicate emotional balance, and if something goes wrong they can lose control.

IMPLICATIONS — WHAT THIS MEANS TO YOU

Angry and hostile customers create a predicament for sales managers. When customers are pushed to this point, something has obviously gone wrong and has not been rectified.

When problems occur, customers want them handled quickly and efficiently. Once done, customers are generally happy with the outcome.

Anger and hostility arise from a lack of care and concern from the sales manager's company. How sales managers and their people set out to resolve a volatile situation will often determine the future of their relationship with the disgruntled customer.

STRATEGIES, TIPS & TECHNIQUES TO APPLY

Salespeople are usually trained to give hostile customers the opportunity to vent their anger. Once the customer has simmered down, the salesperson typically attempts to solve the problem. Often his or her initial response will be, "What would you like me to do?"

Unfortunately, this query will often elicit an even more hostile and unreasonable response because the salesperson has asked a general question with an obvious answer: the customer clearly wants the company to solve his or her problem. In many customers' minds, this question invites a sarcastic answer. Despite any positive intentions, in the end, the salesperson only deepens the customer's anger and hostility.

Sales managers must get their people to refrain from using the aforementioned question when responding to angry customers. A more appropriate and effective response would be, "Under the circumstances, what would be a fair way to resolve this problem to your satisfaction?"

This is more effective because the question does not invite the obvious response. Additionally, it engages the customer by causing him or her to pause, cool down and reflect, and legitimately consider the question.

Undoubtedly, some customers will attempt to take advantage of the situation by raising unreasonable demands. But most rational people will not do this.

Salespeople have a tendency to overreact to these types of situations, feeling that they must move mountains to keep the customer. They might drop prices or offer several substantial concessions to rectify the situation. However, in most circumstances, customers will expect less than the salesperson is prepared to offer.

Therefore sales managers should urge their people to let the customer offer the initial solution (by way of answering the more effective question discussed above). After the customer responds, the salesperson can either accept the answer by agreeing to resolve the problem according to the customer's conditions or attempt to modify it.

Under either scenario, the salesperson has accomplished several things:

- The customer is calmed down.
- The customer has begun to think positively about a possible solution.
- A potentially dangerous situation has been averted.
- A possible solution has been initiated that is acceptable to all parties.

POINTS TO PONDER — SOMETHING TO THINK ABOUT

1. How do you respond to a hostile and angry customer who has a legitimate complaint and has been unable to get it resolved?
2. What approaches have you successfully taken to resolve customer problems to the satisfaction of both the company and the customer?

TRAINING ACTIVITY — APPLICATION & ACTION PLAN

Detail an experience you have had in the past with an angry and hostile customer.

1. What was the problem?
2. What caused the problem?
3. What escalated the problem to the point that the customer became hostile and angry?
4. At what point did you become involved in the problem?
5. What were the customer's demands?
6. What was your approach?
7. How was the problem resolved?
8. What lessons can be derived from this situation?

5

Make It Easy to Complain

Customers are well aware of the time involved in voicing a complaint. Most don't have the desire or time necessary to resolve a problem. Customers can be busy people, and they perceive the problem resolution process as extra, unnecessary work that is stressful and difficult. Many truly wonder if it really is worth their time and energy. Sometimes, in fact, they feel it is easier to walk away than to complain.

IMPLICATIONS — WHAT THIS MEANS TO YOU

Problems and complaints give a company the opportunity to shine. A sales manager's attitude toward customer problems and complaints can work for or against the organization. If the attitude causes his or her people to dissuade customers from complaining, it could cause an ongoing erosion of the company's sales base.

This is important because if customers sense that it will be difficult to place a legitimate complaint, they simply won't complain. In turn, they will quietly switch to a more receptive supplier. If they have no choice but to buy from an inaccessible supplier, they will continue to buy while becoming activists against that supplier. These unsatisfied customers will be quite happy to spread negative information about the sales personnel they have interacted with and the company itself.

Sales managers need to make sure that their customers are free to voice grievances, and that their salespeople see complaints as a positive opportunity. They can use the feedback to improve company operations, strengthen products and develop customer service.

STRATEGIES, TIPS & TECHNIQUES TO APPLY

When customers analyze the complaint process, they often realize personal shortcomings. Many feel unable to express themselves adequately. Others feel uncomfortable, seeing themselves as a potential problem to the sales representative; they wish to complain only to attain the satisfaction they were promised, but simply cannot handle being seen as a nuisance. Some customers may be insecure and cannot get past the discomfort of dealing with unknown individuals. Still others believe it comes down to a "me against them" conflict, feeling that to attain the desired results they must muster up enough courage to aggressively take on the company and its employees.

Sales managers should take the time to think about what it is like to complain to a supervisor. Most would probably begin the process by evaluating their communication skills. Then, time is spent deciding the best way to communicate effectively. No doubt, many experience some sort of fear when thinking about the potential intimidation that comes with confronting a superior. At this point, careful consideration is often necessary to weigh the possible risks versus rewards of making a complaint. Many customers experience the same feelings when they need to complain about a problem.

Sales managers should keep in mind that when customers complain they have specific concerns. These are described below.

Heard and Listened to Respectfully

Customers expect to be treated with respect. They understand problems arise; they just want a timely response that eliminates the problem. Customers also have an idea of what an appropriate response should be; if they fail to get it, more serious problems can occur.

Served Efficiently and Considerately

Customers are not interested in reasons why the problem cannot be resolved. They don't expect to be referred to numerous different people without results. And they certainly don't want to be told they are the cause of the problem or that no other company has experienced the same issues.

Fast Action

Customers expect problems to be handled quickly. Surveys indicate that the faster a supplier can resolve a problem, the more likely they will develop an intensely loyal customer.

An Atmosphere of Mutual Trust

When customers place their trust in a company they expect its people to do everything to resolve a complaint. They made a personal decision and commitment when they initially gave their business to the salesperson. When issues arise, they expect the supplier to show the same level of commitment to resolve the problem.

Important and Valued

Survey after survey has indicated that customers' chief fear is that a salesperson will abandon them immediately after the sale is finalized and thus be absent when a problem occurs.

Customers want to know that their business is important to the salesperson and his or her manager. The actions taken to resolve (or not resolve, as the case may be) a problem, communicate how important they feel the customer is. This crossroad is a critical juncture that can make or break the business relationship.

After coming up with an effective solution, sales managers should keep in mind that closure is just as important as solving the problem. Closure is the final step that ensures a positive resolution to all of the customer's questions, negative attitudes and frustrations; done right, this cements customer satisfaction.

POINTS TO PONDER — SOMETHING TO THINK ABOUT

1. Do you make it easy for your customers to voice their complaints and concerns? What actions do you take?
2. What is your typical attitude toward a customer who complains? Is your attitude reflected in how your salespeople handle the complaint and deal with the customer?

TRAINING ACTIVITY — APPLICATION & ACTION PLAN

Design a plan that meets each of the customer needs discussed in this chapter. Your primary goal should be to have your salespeople never end a complaint-related visit or call before asking customers, "Has your problem or concern been solved to your satisfaction?"

6

The Customer's Moments of Truth

A vendor's response to a customer's expectations and problems determines whether the customer is satisfied, unhappy, ecstatic or angry. It also determines whether a customer will maintain the sales relationship or leave for a more receptive supplier.

IMPLICATIONS — WHAT THIS MEANS TO YOU

Customers are greatly concerned that a salesperson will disappear once the sale has been secured and the money is collected. Potential complications with the product or service leave customers fearing that they will have to solve a problem without the assistance of the salesperson or his or her manager. Unfortunately, this fear is often justified by their experiences with previous salespeople and companies who left them in a lurch.

Sales managers must understand that a proper development of customer knowledge depends on their people accurately identifying what the buyer wants and expects after the sale is made. This is a crucial area of focus that often causes conflict if not carefully attended to.

Salespeople often feel that once they have closed the sale, their job is over; whereas the customer feels the sale is merely a decision making process. For the latter, the real sale begins with the delivery, installation and successful operation of a product or service.

The key for sales managers is to realize that their people might deliver exactly what was promised and still fail to meet the customer's expectations because they neglected to identify or understand what the buyer truly anticipated. The outcome is an unhappy customer, and the salesperson is often puzzled as to why.

STRATEGIES, TIPS & TECHNIQUES TO APPLY

The objective of the sales manager and the company as a whole is to understand and continuously improve their "moments of truth" with customers. The concept of moments of truth was developed by Scandinavian Airlines as a method for gauging their performance with customers. It can be a helpful concept for sales managers and their people to employ.

What Is a Moment of Truth?

Every interaction between a prospective buyer and a company is a moment of truth. Customers have specific expectations about how the sales process should work and how they should be treated. Each step in the process gives the sales manager and his or her people an opportunity to meet or exceed the customer's expectations.

While every prospect or customer contact is a moment of truth, there are six critical moments salespeople should be especially aware of:

- At the time of the sale
- During delivery
- When there is a problem
- When the customer complains
- When the customer faces competitive pressures
- During follow-up calls

The Correlation Between Customer Fears and Moments of Truth

These six moments of truth are when most customers fear vendors will fail them. Sales managers who understand this correlation and know the critical moments of truth in the sales relationship can use this information to their company's advantage. When the manager's salespeople continuously exceed the prospective buyer's expectations, they add value to the product or service being sold. This gives salespeople a real opportunity to shine and solidify competitive immunity.

What Needs to Be Done

Since every step in the sales process provides the vendor with an opportunity to meet or exceed the prospective buyer's expectations, it is important they clearly identify specific criteria for each critical moment of truth before it occurs.

Additionally, salespeople must identify other important moments of truth for the prospective buyer. Once done, they must ask the buyer to pinpoint their specific expectations for each of these moments. Without concretizing these expectations, it will be difficult for salespeople to satisfy and retain the customer.

Long-term relationships are truly enhanced by exceeding expectations, not by simply meeting them. Successful sales managers realize that when their people "take it to the next level" they establish value-added service that ensures sustained customer satisfaction.

POINTS TO PONDER – SOMETHING TO THINK ABOUT

1. Have you thought about or identified moments of truth in the past?
2. What has happened when your people failed to properly handle any one of these critical moments of truth? Give an example.

TRAINING ACTIVITY — APPLICATION & ACTION PLAN

Identify a customer that you consider a typical or average representation of your clientele.

1. Define the key moments of truth in this business relationship.
2. Explain what makes these moments critical.
3. Identify an additional situation where your company lost a customer or sale by failing to meet their expectations.
4. Upon reflection, can you pinpoint the critical moments of truth that may have been overlooked by the salesperson involved? Explain.

7

Are You Hiding Behind the Policy Book?

One thing that can destroy a vendor's credibility faster than anything else is when its people hide behind company policy. When customers have a problem, it infuriates them and makes matters worse when salespeople and representatives cite company policy as the reason for not being able to help resolve an issue.

IMPLICATIONS — WHAT THIS MEANS TO YOU

No company is free from problems and mistakes. However, a delayed or absent resolution blamed on company policy will quickly turn a customer into an activist against the company. Activists will vigorously spread the word about their poor experience to anyone who will listen. These individuals are angry about their poor experiences and will actively work against the vendor's business efforts. They will sometimes even smear a sales manager's personal reputation along with the reputations of any other individuals they may have had contact with during the business relationship.

Unhappy customers usually tell an average of 25 people about their negative experiences with a supplier. Activists, however, will tell many more people, and, depending upon their influence, they have the potential to drastically harm a sales manager's business and even the company's overall reputation.

It is important for sales managers to understand that most customers view company policy as a ruse for not wanting to solve their problem. Customers expect the individuals they deal with to fight for them. They want to see flexibility on the part of the company in crafting a viable and acceptable solution.

Sales managers may win the battle when they rigidly enforce company policy, but will ultimately lose the war when customers take their business elsewhere and/or become activists.

STRATEGIES, TIPS & TECHNIQUES TO APPLY

Most individuals are reasonable: they know that problems are going to happen. When a problem does occur, customers mostly just want it fixed. However, they do expect a quick and timely resolution. The last thing they want to deal with is a bureaucratic sales representative who refuses to resolve their problem and hides behind the company handbook.

Business relationships are built on trust. To the customer, trust means that when there is a problem they expect the vendor and its representatives to quickly resolve it. If a sales manager's company has established enough trust with a customer to secure his or her business, it has likewise established an expectation in the customer's mind that the company will always be supportive, especially during times of trouble.

Difficulties spring up when a company has firm policies in place. Many such policies are initially established to prevent the company from being taken advantage of by unscrupulous customers. But most companies will remain flexible if reasonable solutions are mutually agreed to when a customer problem arises. Indeed, most companies are discovering that business is entirely too competitive to deal cavalierly with their customers.

Sales managers should have their people use an approach similar to this the next time they encounter a customer problem: "Our policy is not to issue a refund after 30 days. However, it's also our policy not to have unhappy customers. What do you consider to be a fair solution to this problem?"

When sales managers encourage this approach, they give their people a starting point for creating a satisfied, happy customer. It demonstrates that the salesperson or representative cares and is willing to listen and ultimately act to resolve the problem. This approach moves the process forward to solve the problem while keeping the customer content and loyal.

Great business relationships are based on trust and personal credibility. Customers expect the people they deal with to fight for them and to make sure their problems are quickly resolved. Hiding behind a policy book only undermines and destroys credibility; once this situation occurs it becomes difficult for a company to ever regain a customer's confidence, loyalty and trust.

POINTS TO PONDER — SOMETHING TO THINK ABOUT

1. How do your people resolve a customer's problem when faced with a firm company policy?
2. How do your people handle retaining a customer who is infuriated by a company policy?

TRAINING ACTIVITY — APPLICATION & ACTION PLAN

Take a few minutes to see your company from the customer's perspective.

1. Does your company have any rules and policies that might appear unreasonable?
2. Identify and pinpoint problem areas.
3. Develop some alternative sales strategies to minimize recurring problems.

8

Customers Would Rather Switch Than Fight

It is much easier for customers to switch suppliers than it is to complain. Customers have become more knowledgeable about products and more demanding when it comes to service. If one company is not fulfilling their needs, it's quite easy to move on to the next.

IMPLICATIONS – WHAT THIS MEANS TO YOU

In the normal course of business, complaints and problems are natural. Typically, a salesperson will receive customer feedback and handle it according to standard procedure. But when a customer offers no feedback, this should send up a red flag. Many customers won't complain, even if there is a legitimate reason. Therefore sales managers need to ensure their people maintain continual contact with customers to anticipate and resolve problems before they turn into crises.

Many sales managers will find that most of their salespeople feel customer silence is golden—that is, until the next order fails to arrive. Only then do most discover that a problem exists. Often, however, it is too late to do anything because the damage has already been done. The present state of business relationships requires that sales managers help their people ferret out customer problems and complaints, resolve any underlying issues and nurture customer satisfaction.

STRATEGIES, TIPS & TECHNIQUES TO APPLY

It is not hard to understand the dilemma for customers who wish to complain but find it difficult. If customers are made to feel that their complaints are viewed in a positive light, they will be more likely to open up and discuss their problems. When this occurs, customer satisfaction increases because problems are quickly identified and solved—before they become major crises.

The sales manager's attitude toward customer complaints can work for or against him or her. The sales manager's attitude will often be reflected in his or her people's attitudes. If their actions dissuade someone from complaining, they could permanently lose that customer. Sales managers must emphasize the benefits customer complaints bring to their company and ensure that their people react to complaints in a positive manner. Sales managers should remember and reinforce that customers really want:

- To be heard and listened to respectfully
- To be served efficiently and considerately
- Fast action to solve their problems
- Their expectations met in an atmosphere of mutual trust
- To believe they are important to the manager's business

Customers themselves don't like the idea of complaining. Most want to be seen as nice people, and tend to feel it goes against their nature to take control and force an issue. Customers often feel awkward and pushy while complaining, which explains why they often fumble for words, get their facts mixed up, or totally lose focus and digress from their original subject. The following are some specific strategies sales managers can implement in their company to help a customer through the complaint process:

- What a customer says and how he or she says it must be given careful attention.
- The customer's behavior and mannerisms should be closely observed.
- One must look for facial expressions, eye contact or tone of voice that suggests the customer's personality type.
    - Timid customers are more withdrawn. Salespeople or repre-

sentatives should thank these customers for bringing the issue to their attention and for assisting them in remedying the situation.

    - Aggressive or preoccupied customers need to be continually reassured that their problems are being taken seriously.

- All customers have ideas. If they are totally frustrated about the problem, they can be asked to identify what they think should be done to resolve the problem and reestablish satisfaction. Active customer input can help solve similar problems or complaints in the future.
    - Salespeople and representatives should listen attentively and take notes when they hear a good idea. In turn, they should tell the sales manager.

POINTS TO PONDER — SOMETHING TO THINK ABOUT

1. How do your people actively probe for and solicit customers about problems and complaints?
2. Do you encourage or discourage complaints? View your answer in relation to your department's customer retention rates.

TRAINING ACTIVITY — APPLICATION & ACTION PLAN

1. Create a list of the past ten problems your company has had with major customers. Note the following factors:
    - Seriousness of the problem
    - Stage of problem when initially identified
    - Actions taken
    - Speed of resolution

- Customer status (retained or lost)

2. Analyze your answers and determine which elements need to be worked on to strengthen your department's future response.

About the Author

Timothy F. Bednarz, Ph.D. is CEO of the American Management Development Group, Inc. For over 20 years he has researched, designed and authored hundreds of learning and development programs used by Fortune 1000 companies.

He is also the author of *Great! What Makes Leaders Great. What They Did, How They Did It and What You Can Learn from It* (2011).

Speaking Availability

Timothy F. Bednarz, Ph.D. is available for speaking engagements for your next meeting or association event. He can be contacted at 800-654-4935 or by e-mail at timothy.bednarz@majorium.com.

Bulk Sales

Bulk sales of this book or any other titles available from Majorium Business Press. Inquiries can be directed to sales@majorium.com, or by phone at 800-6654-4935.

Quick Order Form

Fax orders: 715-342-1118. Send this form.

Telephone orders: Call 800-654-4935 toll-free. Have your credit card ready.

Email orders: sales@majorium.com

Postal orders: Majorium Business Press, 2025 Main Street, Stevens Point, WI 54481, USA.

Please send the following books:

____

____

____

____

Please send more FREE information on:

❑Catalog ❑Speaking/Seminars ❑Mailing Lists ❑Consulting

Name: ____________________________________

Address: __________________________________

City: ____________________ State: _____ Zip: ________

Telephone: ________________________________

Email address: ______________________________

Sales tax: Please add 5.5% for products shipped to Wisconsin addresses.

Shipping by air:

United States: $4.00 for first book and $2.00 for each additional product.

International: $9.00 for first book; $5.00 for each additional product (estimate).

Made in the USA
Monee, IL
04 November 2026

67377580R00026